D1456427

MARK MARTIN
Mark of Excellence

Larry Woody

www.SportsPublishingLLC.com

Publisher: **Peter L. Bannon**
Senior Managing Editor: **Susan M. Moyer**
Art Director: **K. Jeffrey Higgerson**
Developmental Editor: **Lynnette Bogard**
Interior and Cover Designer: **Kenneth J. O'Brien**
Copy Editor: **Cynthia L. McNew**

www.SportsPublishingLLC.com
ISBN: 1-58261-759-7
Printed in the United States

(photo by Action Sports Photography, Inc.)

Table of Contents

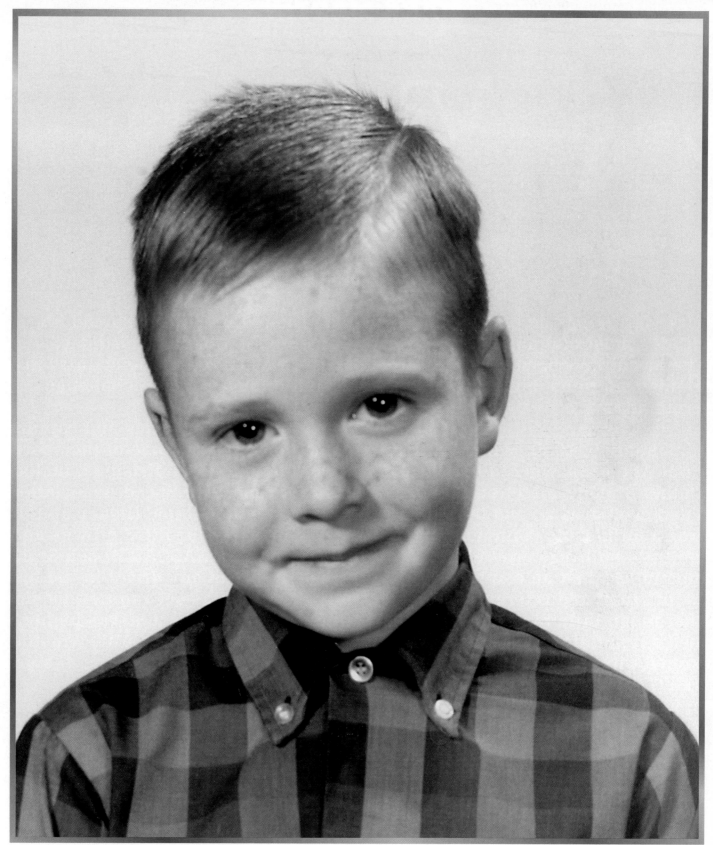

(photo courtesy of Jackie Martin)

Preface

Mark Martin may be one of NASCAR's most diminutive drivers, but he has always been big for his size—big ambitions, big heart, and big determination.

Born January 9, 1959, Martin grew up in rural Arkansas, where he inherited his father Julian's affection for speed and daredevil driving, and by age 15 he was a formidable contender on the tough little bullrings around the area. Competing against an established cadre of crusty old veterans, the leather-tough little racer quickly earned a reputation as a force to be reckoned with. He fought—sometimes literally—and he didn't just hold his own; more often than not, he won.

Martin raced all through high school—on the night of his graduation he had a friend accept his diploma because he was occupied at a racetrack—and it didn't take him long to spread his wings. Before his 20th birthday, Martin was traveling the country in search of bigger racing challenges.

Martin piled up victories and captured championships in some of the sport's lower and mid-level divisions, including four American Speed Association (ASA) championships. Higher up the ladder he won four IROC crowns and collected more NASCAR Busch Series wins—45—than any driver in the history of NASCAR's second-tier division. But always Martin's aim was higher, on the big target: NASCAR's Winston Cup Series, the major league of stock car racing.

He quickly made it, making his first NASCAR Winston Cup start at the tender age of 22. But just as quickly, his boyhood dream began to dissolve into a nightmare as he encountered a series of disheartening setbacks. At one point he found himself so broke that he was forced to sell his race cars and equipment, "down to the last spark plug," and start all over from scratch.

Despondent but not defeated, Martin battled his way back, conquering some personal demons in the process. Helping bolster his spirits was a pretty young woman named Arlene, whom Martin met on a date arranged by his sister. Arlene would eventually become Mrs. Mark Martin and present him with a son, Matt, the light of his life.

Along the way Martin caught the attention of Jack Roush, a prominent race team owner who shared Martin's big ambitions and dreams of competing in the top echelon of NASCAR. Martin and Roush joined forces and after a slow start, quickly picked up momentum and developed into one of the most successful teams in the sport's history.

Still, the going was not always easy. Four times over the years, Martin finished second in the NASCAR Winston Cup championship standings, including a wrenching loss to seven-time champion Dale Earnhardt in a title race decided by a controversial NASCAR points penalty.

But just as in the early days, every time Martin was knocked down he always got back up, brushed himself off, and waded back into the fray.

Obstacles, setbacks and disappointments that would have broken and defeated others only seemed to strengthen and intensify Martin's resolve and determination. They say the hottest fire forges the toughest steel, and that may explain the steely character of the lion-hearted racer. Time and again Martin withstood the toughest tests that an often ruthless sport could throw at him and emerged triumphant.

Mark Martin's story is more than an account of the evolution of a great racer; it is a story of the triumph of the human spirit. It is an inspirational saga of will and perseverance and determination, of a good man who rose from humble beginnings, overcame bad breaks and daunting hurdles, and who in the end stood proud and victorious, both on the racetrack and in the more important race of life.

It has been a remarkable journey by a remarkable man. And it's not over yet.

CHAPTER 1

"Take the Wheel!"

We are sitting in Mark Martin's motor home in the infield of Daytona International Speedway. Inside, the air conditioner hums cool comfort, but outside it is scorching. It is the July 4, 2003 weekend, and Martin is preparing for the upcoming Pepsi 400.

Mark, one of NASCAR's most successful, popular and respected racers, has agreed to take time out of his hectic schedule to meet with a writer and discuss the long, winding path that has brought him to this juncture in his life and his career.

We decide to begin at the beginning.

"Oh, man, it was something," says Martin, his blue eyes sparkling and his face crinkling into a grin as he relates the oft-repeated story of his Batesville, Arkansas, boyhood. "It was

so much fun, so exciting ... gosh, it's hard to describe. It was a blast."

It's almost as though Mark can close his eyes and drift backwards through time, back some four decades, back when he was five years old and sitting on the lap of his father, Julian. A wide-eyed little boy squirming and gasping with excitement as he and his father roar down one of the twisting little back roads that weave their way through rural Arkansas.

"My dad would sit me on his lap and tell me to take the wheel," Martin recalls. "I was too little for my legs to reach the gas and brake pedals, of course, so my dad would mash the gas while I steered. And he'd mash the heck out of it. We'd go tearing along those little winding roads going 70 miles an hour, fish-tailing through the gravel with the dust boiling up

(photo by Action Sports Photography, Inc.)

behind us. We'd come to one of those little narrow bridges and I'd yell for my dad to take the wheel, but he'd just throw back his head, laugh—and speed up. I'd be scared to death, but I'd hang on. I'd grip that wheel as hard as I could and keep steering while my dad was laughing his head off. Oh, man, was it wild."

He pauses, grins and adds:

"Wild and fun. That's the way my dad was."

Julian Martin grew up in Batesville, Arkansas, almost literally behind the wheel of a truck. His father taught him to drive practically before he taught him to walk. Julian married young, having wooed and won a pretty local woman named Jackie Estes, who had a five-year-old daughter named Glenda from a previous marriage. Julian adopted Glenda, and on January 9, 1959, the couple had their first and only child, Mark.

"Glenda and I were very close," Martin says. "We were just a typical brother and sister. We played together, did a lot of kid stuff together. We were best friends."

Their enterprising father began a trucking business to support his family, making runs to Memphis and St. Louis to deliver goods and produce. Mark constantly tagged at the heels of the father he adored.

"Wherever he went, I went," Martin says. "I was like his little shadow."

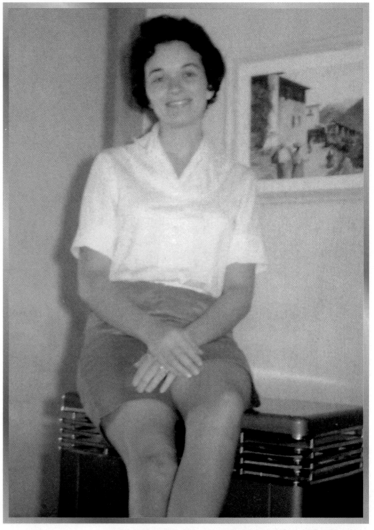

Jackie Martin (photo courtesy of Jackie Martin)

Martin describes himself as a "typical small-town kid," playing Little League baseball and riding his bicycle around the neighborhood. Even as a tyke on a bike, Mark took his driving seriously. He tended to ride his bike faster than the other kids. His genes were showing.

"I've always been competitive," he says. "Anything I've ever done, I've gone at it 100 percent. I don't know any other way."

Mark's craving for speed, his competitive desire, was inherited. Julian liked to ride fast, too, slinging his car around the curves and occasionally challenging his buddies to drag races. Julian was a fan of fast cars and fast driving, and naturally that made him

Julian and Mark Martin at the Gulf when Mark was six years old. (photo courtesy of Jackie Martin)

an avid racing fan. He owned part interest in a race car that competed on a local track, and Mark often attended races with his father, hanging out in the pits.

"Those are some of my earliest memories," Mark says. "Going to the track with my dad. We'd go down in the pits, close to the action, and it was really exciting. I remember the dust and the fumes and the roar of the cars. I was attracted to it. Even as a little kid, I felt right at home in that environment."

In addition to following area racing, Julian also enjoyed attending big-league NASCAR spectacles, and in 1973 he took Mark along with him to the Daytona 500.

Young Mark remembers the experience as "incredible," and he was immediately hooked.

"I don't remember pulling for any particular driver back then," he says. "I don't know that my dad had a particular favorite, either. Shoot, I liked 'em all. I think he just liked racing in general. That's pretty much how I remember it."

And as young Martin watched, something whispered in his ear over the roar of the engines: "This is your des-

tiny. Someday you will race in NASCAR. Someday you will compete at Daytona. Someday …"

When Mark and his father returned home from Daytona, Martin began to badger his dad to build him a race car.

Julian Martin (photo courtesy of Jackie Martin)

"My dad had always tinkered with cars, working on them, making them go fast," Mark says. "He knew a lot of guys who had used cars, and somewhere he acquired a six-cylinder '55 Chevy and converted it into a stock car. He made the roll bars out of water pipes. We painted the car bright orange with a No. 2 on the side. Oh, boy, was it beautiful. My dad had done a super job with it, making it look sharp, and was I ever proud of that baby!"

Mark Martin, barely 15, was ready to go racing. He had a destiny to chase, and he was itching to get started.

There was just one hitch. He wasn't old enough for a driver's license. No problem. Julian would drive him to the local track—Independence County Speedway in nearby Locust Grove, Arkansas—towing their race car behind them.

"I guess that may sound kinda strange to some folks, but back then kids started driving long before they got their license," Martin says. "It wasn't unusual. But going racing at that age ... yeah, I guess THAT was a little different. But somehow it seemed natural to me. My father seemed confident that I could do it, and I guess his confidence rubbed off on me. And so we loaded up our race car and away we went."

Under the track rules, an underage driver could compete if his parents signed a consent form. Julian signed and Mark raced. A family friend, Larry Shaw, joined the effort, helping maintain the race car. They gave their humble operation a lofty name: The Mark Martin Racing Team.

"Larry was a local mechanic who enjoyed working on cars and also enjoyed racing," Martin says. "He was a big help, as were some other local

> ## "My Dad was my hero. He did very little wrong in my eyes. He did almost everything right."
> ### —Mark Martin on the influence of his father

guys, friends of my father's. A number of guys pitched in and helped us out."

Martin ran his first stock car race on April 19, 1974, on Locust Grove's little quarter-mile dirt oval. It was a rough track, with bumps and humps and potholes. Sometimes when a tire hit a pothole, the jolt would almost jerk the steering wheel from Martin's tiny fists. But he just grunted, gritted his teeth, and held on. Just like his daddy taught him.

"It was an extremely rough race track," Martin says, "but what did I know about it? Heck, I didn't know any different. That's the only kind of track I'd ever been on. I figured that if you were going to race, this was the kind of track you raced on."

There was a decided streak of bulldog developing in the young driver. During one memorable race, Martin's car hit a chuckhole in the middle of a turn, and it jolted so violently that it swerved out of control. Martin's bright orange Chevy swerved off the track, went over the dirt berm that served as a retaining wall, and disappeared from sight. Martin never let off the gas. Suddenly he popped back over the berm at the far end, bounced back onto the track, and—trailing weeds and grass—kept right on going.

"Like I said, it was pretty wild," Martin says, smiling at the memory. "There was never a dull moment when you were on that track."

Watching from the pits, Mark's mom gasped. His dad just grinned. Atta boy. Hang onto it. Don't let up. Keep going!

Julian once proudly told a friend when discussing his son's racing style: "He's an aggressive little cuss."

Mark took it as a compliment of the highest order.

"I didn't like to lose," he says. "Not even back then."

*L*ocust Grove, with its mud, bumps, potholes and rough-hewn cadre of local good ol' boys, was a long way from Daytona. But as far as Martin was concerned, it was pure heaven.

"To this day I remember how exciting it was," he says. "Of course I didn't know what I was doing out there—I was just a kid with no racing experience or knowledge. Go fast and turn left, that was about it. I was operating on pure instinct and with what general instructions my father was able to give me.

"But it sure was fun, and the more I raced the more I enjoyed it. It was all I thought about. I'd go to school during the day and as soon as I got home I'd start tinkering on my race car. When my dad got home from work, he'd join me. It was all my mom could do to get us to stop and come in for supper."

He pauses and smiles.

"I treasure those memories."

Julian in front of one of the trucks that Mark piloted as a child. (photo courtesy of Jackie Martin)

That spring and summer Martin competed at Independence County Speedway and at the Speed Bowl in Benton, Arkansas. He kept careful notes and records of each race—where he started, how he ran, where he finished. The record shows that Martin won 22 times in 101 starts and captured a victory in what was billed as an Arkansas State Championship race.

"I've always [taken] a businesslike approach to my racing," Martin says. "From the very start I tried to learn and to apply what I learned to the next race."

Mark and his "best friend" and sister Glenda. (photo courtesy of Jackie Martin)

In the process of getting a race track education, Martin also began to capture a great deal of attention—of different varieties. Local newspapers took note of the hot young racing phenom, and he stared receiving glowing write-ups. However, some of Martin's race track competition didn't respond to his accomplishments quite so glowingly.

Veteran drivers didn't cotton to the idea of being beaten by a 15-year-old kid who looked more like ten. At the time, Martin stood five feet tall on his tiptoes and weighed less than 100 pounds soaking wet. He possessed an innocent boyish face right out of a Norman Rockwell painting. Hardly the image of the rugged racer who was wreaking havoc on the local racetrack.

Also stirring resentment among some of his rivals was the fact that Martin drove a sleek, well-groomed, carefully maintained race car—at least compared to some of the dented clinkers in which the opposition often competed.

"I was a kid with a nice-looking car who was winning a lot of races," Martin says. "There was a lot of resentment and jealousy. Drivers by nature are a pretty proud lot with big egos, and some of the veterans didn't like losing to a kid. I got a lot of hard stares and heard a lot of muttering."

Sometimes it went further than just muttering.

"I remember one guy who got so mad at getting beat that he quit racing," Martin says. "Just up and quit, rather than keep racing against me. Another guy had been beating and banging on me, and one night I came up behind him and took him out. I hit him in the

> **"We all said that, when he first started racing, he's going to win the Daytona 500 by the time he's 25."**
> —Jackie Martin on Mark's success at such an early age

17

rear—bang!—and he went spinning. I guess I had a little bit of a temper, too. I don't recall him bothering me much after that."

Sputtering and swapping sheet metal was about as far as most of Martin's peeved rivals dared to go. Julian had a reputation as a tough, no-nonsense fellow who took nothing from nobody. Suffice it to say, he didn't acquire all those scars on his knuckles from working on race cars. It would not have been prudent to pick on his son.

"It was as rough off the track as it was on it," Martin says. "You had to be tough to survive back then, and my father was tough. Most of the guys were afraid to mess with him too much."

Another grin.

"Let's just say that he was not particularly subtle in his approach to solving problems."

And so, as the competition continued to choke on young Martin's dust that summer, all they could do was growl and bear it. The kid wouldn't give them an inch.

"It was important to establish yourself, let people know that you wouldn't take anything off of them," Martin says. "I didn't want to get a reputation as a driver who would back off or back down. I wasn't going to let anybody intimidate me. I was determined to hold my own out there."

As tough as Martin was on the race track, his personality was just the opposite when the engines were turned off and the roar subsided. As the engines cooled, so did young Mark's temperament. He was generally regarded as "quiet" and seldom was involved in mischief.

"I didn't get into much trouble as a kid," Martin says, adding with a smile: "Maybe it was because I was so consumed by racing that I didn't have time to get into anything. I was too busy. But really, I never was the kind of kid who needed to be spanked or disciplined. I didn't want to do anything that would upset and disappoint my parents. I always wanted them to be proud of me."

The Martin family's home life, however, was not idyllic. Jackie divorced Julian, who had a penchant for recklessness. They remarried. And separated again. His parents' unstable relationship did not seem to affect Martin. He felt close to both his mother and his father, despite their sometimes rocky relationship.

"I always knew that I had their love and their support," Martin says. "And I had my racing. That was all I needed. Sure, there were some rocky times, but overall, I look back on my boyhood with nothing but fond memories."

(photo courtesy of Jackie Martin)

Mark Martin and Dick Trickle circa 1987 at Ohio's Queen City Speedway. (photo by Christopher Denny)

CHAPTER 2

Moving on up

Mark Martin wasn't content to be the proverbial big duck on a small pond, and he quickly grew restless on the dusty little bull rings around his home in Batesville. He needed bigger worlds to conquer, and so he began to branch out in search of stronger challenges, traveling all the way to Springfield, Missouri, some 200 miles away, to test his racing mettle.

"I had done pretty well on my home track," he says, "and I was anxious to prove myself somewhere else. I needed some new challenges and opportunities."

On the night of his high school graduation, Martin was not on hand to accept his diploma. Instead, he was racing in Springfield, where he set a track qualifying record. A friend picked up his diploma for him.

"I had already decided that racing was what I wanted to do for the rest of my life," Martin says. "School didn't interest me. Racing was the only thing I cared about. I was getting my 'education' on the race track."

That didn't mean he was a poor student. Martin proved he could hit the books with the best of them—with the proper incentive. During his senior year he made a deal with his father that if he made the honor roll he could skip graduation and go racing. He made the honor roll.

"Again, it was a case of me wanting my parents to be proud of me," Martin says. "Also, it was the best way to get to go racing. That was all the incentive I needed."

Martin became acquainted with Larry Phillips, a top driver at Springfield's

(photo courtesy of Jackie Martin)

Fairgrounds Speedway. Phillips was a veteran racer who knew the sport well. Like others who witnessed Martin's racing performances, he became more and more impressed with the tough little battler from Batesville. Phillips offered Martin a job at his racing shop in Springfield following high school graduation.

"Larry was another one of those people who was very instrumental to my early racing career," Martin says. "He helped me a great deal. I was still learning. I

Already with an ASA Championship under his belt at a young age, Mark poses beside his team's truck in the late 1970s. Notice the Dennis the Menace-like figure on the truck has an ASA Champion patch on his uniform along with Mark's ASA car number 2. (photo by Dick Conway)

was eager to learn, and Larry was a good teacher."

That was Martin's version of higher education: working on race cars and building parts in Phillips's shop. It was hard, dirty work, but Martin never complained. Whatever task he was assigned, he completed. Phillips considered Mark a diligent, dependable worker who never shirked a task.

Through the week Mark worked on race cars; on weekend nights he raced them.

That summer, in 1977, he suffered his first serious crash and injury. He was screaming around the fast, high banks of I-70 Speedway in Odessa, Missouri, when he spun and hit the wall hard. He suffered a chipped bone in his shoulder.

"What do I remember about it?" Martin says with a shrug. "I remember that it hurt. It hurt badly. But it didn't scare me. I realized even back then that wrecks and injuries and pain are all a part of it. I'd been around racing enough to understand that. It didn't scare me or intimidate me in the least."

The next weekend Martin was right back on the track—aching shoulder and all—not only racing but winning yet another race.

Later that season Martin crashed again on the same track. This time he was left with a dislocated toe that put him on crutches.

"Pain is part of it," Martin shrugs. "You learn to live with it, deal with it, drive with it. You put it out of your mind and go on."

Martin, accustomed to the slower speeds on the little dirt tracks, had to adjust to the gripping asphalt and its higher speeds, not to mention the hard concrete retaining walls. Unlike his home track at Locust Grove, where he could sail off the track and dart right back on, at Odessa there were barriers. Unforgiving barriers.

The learning experience, as painful as it was, continued. Young Martin was dented but undeterred and bursting with ambition.

That spring he told a sports writer about his grand plan: "I want to win the Daytona 500 ... and win it before I'm 25."

Martin afterward admitted that he was "somewhat embarrassed" to see his boast in print, but he didn't take it

Mark sitting on his ASA car before qualifying in the late 1970s with longtime crew chief David Lovendahl in the background. Lovendahl later went to work at Petty Enterprises. After Mark failed to make it in NASCAR Winston Cup competition the first time, he went back to ASA. When he came back to NASCAR, it was in a NASCAR Busch Series car in 1987 owned by Lovendahl's brother-in-law, Bruce Lawmaster. (photo by Dick Conway)

back. He was on a roll, he was learning and progressing, and as he noted at the time, he had seven years to reach his goal. A Daytona 500 victory in seven years? Why not?

"I was young, I'd had a lot of success up to that point, and I had a lot of self-confidence and faith in my ability," he says.

Martin didn't consider himself a cocky driver, just a confident one. As he said, he had confidence in his driving ability, confidence in his race cars, confidence in the people around him. A reporter had asked him a simple question and Martin had given an honest answer. A brash answer, perhaps, but honest and straightforward. That sort of complete candidness, a willingness to speak his mind, would continue to be his trademark.

Later in 1977 Martin began competing in the American Speed Association (ASA) Series. The ASA featured many of the best short-track racers in the Midwest—veterans like Dick Trickle, Bob Strait, Mike Eddy and a promising newcomer from St. Louis named Rusty Wallace.

Wallace and Martin came up through the ASA ranks together, entered NASCAR together, and today share the distinction of being among the sport's most successful racers.

Wallace, reflecting on their many years together in the sport, says he has always been not just a rival of Martin's, but a fan and a friend as well.

"I admire the heck out of Mark," Wallace says. "Ever since I've known him—and that covers a whole lot of years—he has been a consistently class act. I guess the thing that stands out most in my mind about him is his determination. There's never been a tougher racer than Mark Martin. No matter what he's racing in—ASA, NASCAR Busch Series, NASCAR Winston Cup—he'll do his damndest to beat you. He'll run the damn tires right off his race car, then race you on the rims. I really admire that. He has always been one helluva driver. Mark Martin is a racer's racer."

The ASA meant widespread exposure and even tougher competition. To Martin, that translated into advancement and opportunity. He welcomed the challenge. He thrived on it.

Rex Robbins, the ASA president, recognized natural talent when he saw it, and as far as he was concerned,

Darrell Waltrip, a rising racing star in Franklin, Tennessee, explained his predicament, and asked Waltrip to drive the car for him. Waltrip agreed.

"I had become well acquainted with Mark and really admired him," says Waltrip. "I was glad to help him out any way I could."

Waltrip would go on to become one of the sport's all-time greats. He won three NASCAR Winston Cup championships and 84 races—tied for third all-time—by the time he retired at the end of the 2000 season. Today he is part of the Fox Network's award-winning NASCAR broadcasting team and remains a devout friend and fan of Martin.

"To me, Mark represents everything our sport is about," Waltrip says. "First of all, he is a genuinely good guy, a true class act. On the track, he is an extremely talented race driver and a tough competitor. I don't know that anybody out there races harder than Mark, lap after lap. He's worked hard, paid a lot of dues, and I'm happy for his success. Everything he's got, he's worked hard for it. He's earned it."

Even after securing Waltrip as a temporary relief driver, the Martins' troubles weren't over. Mark and his father Julian were en route to LaCrosse, towing their race car, when Julian was seriously injured in a freak accident.

They had stopped at a service station in Illinois when a passing motorist pulling a boat lost a wheel. The wheel bounced off the road and struck Julian on the hand and leg, breaking a finger and dislocating his knee. He was rushed to a hospital, treated, and released. In agonizing pain, Julian rejoined his son and they continued on their way—both hobbled and hurting.

The next day they arrived at the race track, Mark in a wheelchair with casts on both feet and Julian on crutches.

Waltrip recalls: "They were a pitiful-looking pair. But they were determined for me to run their car in that race. I told them I'd do the very best job possible for them. I remember they had a really good race car—very fast and very smooth, and they did a great job of getting it set up."

The only hitch was the size of the cockpit, which had been designed for the diminutive Martin, making it a tight fit for the considerably more bulky Waltrip. But Waltrip, who was already building a national reputation as one of the sport's top racers, somehow made it. He beat the venerable

A young Mark Martin in the pits with two NASCAR legends, David Pearson and short track ace Butch Lindley, a two-time NASCAR Sportsman Series champion. Butch Lindley eventually died in 1990 after being in a coma, since 1985, that he sustained from racing injuries in a crash at Bradenton, Florida. (photo by Dick Conway)

Dick Trickle to take the checkered flag, and in Victory Circle an exhausted Waltrip was joined by Mark in his wheelchair and Julian on his crutches.

"I guess if you looked at the 'victory celebration' and saw the winners, you had to wonder, 'What about the OTHER guys?'" Waltrip recalls with a chuckle. "We were a pretty beat-up-looking bunch."

Three weeks later, Martin went back to his doctor and ordered him to cut the cast off his leg. He was determined to get back behind the wheel. The doctor grudgingly consented, but with a dire warning: If Martin was involved in another crash, the unhealed leg would surely break again.

"I told him to go on and get it off," Martin says. "I'd worry about that when the time came."

Because of his fractured left foot, Martin was unable to work the clutch pedal. He got around the problem by installing a hand clutch in his car, and headed off to race in Milwaukee. He started the weekend off by winning the pole with a track record qualifying lap. Then he proceeded to win one of the most brutal races of his life.

Martin endured excruciating pain throughout the race, and when it was over he had to be helped from his race car. A crewman noticed blood oozing through Martin's casts and bandages.

Pain: the racer's constant companion. But Mark had persevered. He had raced and he had won, and he had retained the points lead in his drive for a third straight ASA championship.

Martin didn't let up. From Milwaukee he went to Indianapolis Raceway Park, where he set a track record—his first of five down the season's stretch—and captured victories at Salem, Indiana, and Odessa, Missouri. Pure grit and the assistance of a young crew chief named Banjo Grimm had carried Martin to yet another title.

"I was hot and I was on a roll," Martin says. "I was in one of those grooves that a driver and a team gets into sometimes, where the car is working great and everything seems to be going your way. Those are the times when it's fun to be a racer."

At 21, Martin was nationally recognized as a short track terror. He was the undisputed king of the ASA. But he wasn't satisfied. The ASA was a spirited, competitive series, but it was-

Mark at Queen City Speedway in Ohio, circa 1987. (photo by Christopher Denny)

n't NASCAR. It was not the peak of the profession.

"I knew exactly where I wanted to go," Martin says. "I had known for a long time—NASCAR Winston Cup. Now I felt like I was ready to make the move."

And so the following season, 1981, Mark Martin—tested, seasoned and battle-scarred at 22—kicked open the door and barged into the NASCAR big leagues.

Mark's ASA car in 1987. (photo by Christopher Denny)

CHAPTER 3

Triumph and Turmoil

Perhaps it was appropriate that Mark Martin should make his NASCAR Winston Cup debut at North Wilkesboro Speedway, a tough little track, fitting for a tough little driver.

North Wilkesboro, nestled in the mountains of North Carolina, has since been dropped from the NASCAR NEXTEL Cup schedule in favor of more illustrious, urban venues like Las Vegas, St. Louis and Chicago. But in its prime, North Wilkesboro was part of stock car racing's soul and culture. It lies in the heart of moonshine country, and moonshine runners were the original Southern stock car racers.

In the sport's early days, drivers would gather to race their "liquor" cars against each other to compare speeds and test their driving skills. As word got out about these bragging-rights "competitions"—usually held in some remote cow pasture—crowds would gather to watch. Someone had an idea: Put up a few benches for the spectators to sit on and charge admission.

The sport of stock car racing was born.

Eventually race tracks were built to house the competition, with North Wilkesboro Speedway being one of the originals. It was there that Martin ran his first big-league NASCAR race.

Martin was not intimidated by the track nor by the veteran NASCAR Winston Cup drivers who convened there—racing legends like Richard Petty, Cale Yarborough and Bobby Allison. In his first attempt at making a NASCAR Winston Cup race, Martin not only cracked the starting lineup, he qualified an impressive fifth.

Sitting with his Apache Stoves crew prior to a 1982 NASCAR Winston Cup race. Things were more casual in those days, with drivers hanging out in the pits and not sequestered in haulers and motor coaches. (photo by Dick Conway)

(photo by Dick Conway)

And so, on an overcast afternoon on April 3, 1981, Martin rolled to the line to take the starting flag for his first NASCAR Winston Cup race.

"I don't remember being tense or tight or anything like that," Martin says of his big debut. "By that time I had been racing several years in other divisions, against some awfully tough drivers. I hadn't had any NASCAR Winston Cup experience, but I'd been in a lot of races that were just as competitive and challenging, against some pretty darned good competition."

Spring showers had struck shortly before race time, and with mist shrouding the mountains, NASCAR officials elected to start under a yellow-green flag—under caution, but with the laps counting. Instead of being able to thunder away with the adrenaline pumping, Martin was forced to creep along for several laps, giving the tension time to seep in and nibble at his nerves.

Once the race started for real, Martin's car lasted only 166 laps before it lost a cylinder. The rear end of his car also burned out, and he found himself engulfed in smoke. His early exit was hardly the stuff of dreams.

But even though it was not a dream start, it was a start, nevertheless. Martin was an official NASCAR Winston Cup racer.

His next NASCAR Winston Cup effort came at Nashville Speedway, like North Wilkesboro an historical old track located at the state Fairgrounds. Nashville, like North Wilkesboro, has since been snipped from the circuit. Once again Martin made an impressive qualifying run—sixth fastest among the field of veterans—only to once again be knocked out of the race with mechanical problems.

"It was pretty frustrating," Martin says. "I knew that I could drive the car if the car would just hold up. But mechanical problems are something that's out of the driver's control. You can't let it get you down. You try to correct the problems and hope they don't keep popping up."

Martin didn't mope. He went home and worked on his car, determined to exorcise the gearbox gremlins that had been harassing him. He had no "insider" assistance, no technical advisors to offer advice. He had a crew that was as young and inexperienced as the driver, and they were forced to feel their way along and figure out their problems on their own.

"We were basically learning as we went," he says. "There was lots of trial and error to what we were doing."

A couple of months later, Martin returned to Nashville for the track's second NASCAR Winston Cup race of the season and this time—in just his third start—he won the pole.

Reporters on hand for the July 11 race were familiar with Martin's name through his ASA exploits and recall how professional the 22-year-old appeared during the biggest moment of his fledgling career.

A beaming Martin held his trophy aloft and said, "You always remember your first pole. This is real special for me and my race team."

Martin won the pole for the Busch Nashville 420 with a lap of 20.561 seconds—104.353 mph—around the five-eighths-mile speedway. That was 1.41 seconds faster than second-place Ricky Rudd.

A beaming Martin told reporters:

"In the NASCAR Winston Cup race tomorrow night, I just want to be a good, strong competitor ... I told everybody this would be a good week for me here."

Those on hand at Nashville Raceway that night remember Martin's excitement as he bathed in the spotlight. His eyes sparkled as he chatted with members of the media. He was clearly a man on a mission, and he had just completed his first objective of that mission. He had won his first NASCAR Winston Cup pole.

The race was run at night, under the lights, but even so, the mid-July heat was brutal. Richard Petty always claimed that Nashville was the hottest track on the NASCAR circuit, noting that the track is built down in a depression where little air circulates.

Not only was the night sweltering, the length of the race—420 laps—was much longer than in the ASA events to which Martin was accustomed.

"When you're used to running relatively shorter races, all those extra laps can take a toll," Martin says. "It's like anything else—you have to get your mind and body conditioned to it."

When the starting flag fluttered, Martin, fresh and feisty, jetted into the lead and stayed out front for 36 laps.

Mark gets loose and scrapes the guardrail at the old Richmond Fairgrounds half-mile track in a 1982 NASCAR Winston Cup race. Mark had carried the number 2 on his ASA cars, and since it was already taken by another team in NASCAR Winston Cup, he ran the 02.
(photo by Dick Conway)

Mark, circa 1988. (photo by Dick Conway)

But gradually his car's handling began to go away—critical on the tight little five-eighths-mile oval—forcing Martin to work harder and harder as he wrestled his cranky car through the turns.

With the heat building up and his car becoming more and more stubborn, Martin began to fall off the pace. Soon the leaders passed him. Then he lost another lap. And another ... at the end of the race he was five laps down.

Although Martin termed the experience "humiliating," the record shows that he finished a respectable 11th, well ahead of some of the greatest drivers in the sport at that time.

Wilting in the heat was nothing to be ashamed of; the blistering temperatures took a toll on even the most seasoned drivers. Darrell Waltrip, who won the race, had grown up on the Nashville track, winning two championships and holding the record for most wins there in the weekly NASCAR racing series. Yet after the race, the heat overcame even Waltrip. Suffering from cramps and exhaustion, he had to be helped into the press box, where he conducted his interview lying on his back with an oxygen mask over his face. Waltrip also suffered a burn on his heel that was so serious it later required a bone graft.

Harry Hyde, the colorful character after whom the crew chief's character was patterned in the movie *Days of Thunder*, was working with Martin that race. Hyde said Martin's problems were compounded by having set his seat too far back in the car.

Hyde explained to reporters that Martin had adjusted the car to make it comfortable in practice and when he was simply sitting in the car. Having never run a race that long, Martin failed to understand that as the race went on, the pull and the forces keep pushing the driver sideways and backwards. It wasn't long before he was having trouble reaching the pedals.

"It was a work in progress," Martin says of his early NASCAR Winston Cup career. "I was racing, and learning as I went along. Each race I ran was a new lesson learned."

Martin was not discouraged. He continued to compete in ASA races and also captured an ARCA victory in his first trip to giant Talladega Superspeedway. Martin ran his fourth NASCAR Winston Cup race in September at Richmond (Virginia) International Raceway and won another pole, but again was plagued by mechanical problems once the race started. He was two laps down at the finish, but still salvaged a decent seventh. Then it was on to Martinsville Speedway, where he led 39 laps and finished third. He wasn't in contention for the win—he was three laps down at the finish—but he had posted his best finish in NASCAR's top division.

The 1981 season ended with Martin having won $13,950 for his five NASCAR Winston Cup races. He finished 42nd in the standings.

"Not great, but not bad, either, for someone just starting out," Martin says. "I felt pretty good. I'd gained a lot of experience, learned a lot of valuable lessons. I felt like I was making good progress."

Martin spent the winter mapping plans for his first full NASCAR Winston Cup season in 1982, with a goal of winning Rookie of the Year. In the process he decided to make a total commitment, moving to Charlotte, North Carolina, the heart of NASCAR country. He hired a new crew chief and landed a sponsorship for $50,000—not huge compared to the budgets of most other NASCAR Winston Cup teams, but at least it was a start.

Martin rolled into Daytona in February for Speedweeks, brimming with excitement and anticipation. He had already qualified for the preliminary NASCAR Busch Clash thanks to his Nashville pole the previous July—the first rookie ever to make the Clash field—and brought his car home in eighth place. He was off to a good start.

But then things started to turn sour.

> **"I was racing against Richard Petty, Bobby Allison and Darrell Waltrip, and they didn't look like they were going to be that hard to beat to me."**
> **—Mark Martin on his first year in NASCAR Winston Cup racing in 1981**

Mark walks through the pits at Oxford Plains, Maine, in 1987. Notice the dirt versus the concrete garage areas of today.
(photo by Dick Conway)

Martin's car was not set up properly for the 2.5-mile, aerodynamically challenging Daytona track, and he qualified 26th—a humbling experience for a youngster who the year before had won two poles in five attempts. He never got up to speed in the race, and after just 75 laps his engine blew. He finished 30th.

Shortly afterwards, his crew chief was released. On top of that, the sponsorship money failed to come through.

Martin left Daytona broke and dejected. His big boyhood dream of racing at Daytona had turned into a nightmare. Things seemed to be unraveling around him.

He was, in his own words, "broke, both in spirit and financially."

The season continued to go downhill from there. Martin's car continued to be haunted by mechanical problems. He struggled through race after race. By the July midway point of the season when the NASCAR Winston Cup circuit swung through Nashville—site of Martin's big pole triumph the previous year—Martin's team was in a shambles.

"There was a lot of turmoil," Martin recalls. "It was a very difficult time."

Martin, unable to collect his sponsorship money, was not the only one having financial problems. His father Julian's trucking company also had fallen on hard times. Amid all that, just when the family thought the situation couldn't become any more grim, it did: Martin's transporter was involved in a crash on the way to a race in Atlanta and virtually totaled. More expenses for a team already financially strapped.

Martin doggedly plugged along. Despite all the headaches and setbacks, he managed to finish 14th in the 1982 point standings and win $126,665. But the prized Rookie of the Year title he so badly desired eluded him. Geoffrey Bodine took home the trophy.

"I just got swallowed up that season," Martin later confided. "Things got started going downhill, and we couldn't seem to get it stopped."

Longtime friend Darrell Waltrip suggested that Martin should drop back to a part-time schedule and regroup, but Martin didn't take the advice. He did elect to make one major change, however. During the off season he decided that he would give up trying to be an

Mark being interviewed by Joe Kelley, a longtime track announcer in Virginia and North Carolina, after a 1987 NASCAR Busch Series win at Orange County Speedway in Rougemont, North Carolina. (photo by Dick Conway)

Mark manages to stay out of a spin at Martinsville, Virginia in March 1989 involving Chuck Bown #63 and Martin Truex #58.
Martin Truex, Jr. currently drives for the Chance 2 Team owned by Teresa Earnhardt and Dale Earnhardt, Jr.
(photo by Dick Conway)

owner/driver and concentrate on racing for someone else.

It was a painful decision to give up The Mark Martin Race Team, the team he had begun building at age 15. But in the spring of 1983, he posted the auction notice. Everything he owned—his cars, his tools, his trailers, his parts—was for sale.

"I had put so much work, so much of my heart into that team," Martin says. "It really hurt to have to let it go, but I had no choice. It's still painful to think about."

On April 2, 1983, the auctioneer's gavel fell on Mark Martin's heart.

During the off season, having made up his mind to sell his team, Martin signed to drive for J.D. Stacey. But after a so-so start in the '83 season, Martin was released. He served a brief stint as a driver for D.K. Ulrich and finished the season running a partial schedule for Morgan-McClure Racing.

Martin ran a total of 16 races that season, and when it ended he was not sure where his next ride was coming from—or even if there would be a next ride.

Depressed and dejected, Martin entered into a dark period. Trying to escape his troubles and problems, he began drinking heavily. That was unusual for Martin, who at one time had been kidded by his buddies for barely sipping a beer.

"I had never liked alcohol because of my dad's drinking," Martin would later confide to friends. "I had seen what it could do. It destroyed my parents' marriage. I loved my dad, but when he drank he'd become volatile, and it scared me. I promised myself that I'd never be like that."

> **"He had a very short fuse and was incredibly powerful. No one messed with my dad...no one. I was very scared when he was upset."**
>
> **—Mark Martin on his father**

Martin initially began drinking "socially." But once he started, he found it hard to stop.

"I was depressed and bitter over my racing deal," he said. "But that's no excuse. If you want an excuse to drink, you can always find one, and I sure found mine."

It was a tortured, tormented time for a young man who had always been good-natured and trouble-free and who had had such a positive outlook on life. Mark was in danger of adding a shattered life to a shattered dream.

Martin had reached a low ebb in both his career and his life. He desperately needed something good and positive to happen, and it did, in a double dose. First, he met a pretty young woman named Arlene, and later he was introduced to an ambitious race team owner named Jack Roush.

They would get Martin back on track— literally and figuratively—and change his life forever.

Mark winning his first NASCAR Busch Series race at Dover in 1987. Rusty Wallace is in the #90 car and Ken Bouchard is in the #10 car. Mark won that race beating Larry Pearson, that year's NASCAR Busch Series champion. (photo by Dick Conway)

CHAPTER 4

A Blind Date Opens His Eyes

Being a famous race driver didn't help Mark Martin land a date with a pretty young woman he met through his sister—in fact, it almost prevented it.

"Racing didn't have an especially good reputation back then," recalls Arlene Martin with a smile. "I had never been interested in racing, didn't know anything about racing, didn't care anything about racing. And I certainly wasn't interested in meeting a race car driver."

It was 1983, and Arlene had enough on her mind already. She was recently divorced and the mother of four.

"Dating anybody right then was not something I cared about," she says.

Arlene grew up in Gainesville, Florida, and moved to Arkansas to attend

Harding College. It was during that period that she became friends with Glenda Martin, Mark's sister.

"Glenda and I were good friends, and she kept after me to come and meet her brother," Arlene recalls. "I kept putting her off, and putting her off but she was very persistent. Finally, I gave in and agreed to come over to their house for dinner one evening."

Arlene was aware that Mark was a race driver, and she admits that she had some preconceived notions about him—all negative.

"As I said, I didn't have a high opinion of racing at the time," she says. "I've really never been athletic-minded. I wouldn't have been swept off my feet if Mark had been a famous football player or basketball player, either, for that matter. But Glenda kept insisting that I meet him, and finally I did."

Was she surprised? Quite pleasantly.

"To be honest, I was expecting some arrogant guy, all full of himself, and as it turned out, Mark was just the opposite," she recalls. "He was very quiet and reserved—almost shy—but very nice and polite. We talked awhile and began to hit it off, just as friends. When I left that evening he asked if he could call me sometime, and I said sure. Again, I thought of it as just a friendship and nothing more."

Mark called. And called. And called.

"We'd talk on the phone for maybe an hour or two at a time," Arlene says. "It was just general conversation; he wanted to know how I was doing and so on. I enjoyed it.

"Then he began to come home for frequent visits—he was living in Wisconsin at the time—and every time he came home he'd ask to see me," Arlene says. "After a couple of months I realized that he wasn't coming home just to visit his folks; he was coming home to see me."

What had begun as a friendship began to blossom into something much more.

(photo by Action Sports Photography, Inc.)

Mark invited Arlene to go with him to the 1984 Daytona 500, and she agreed.

"It was the first race I had been to in my life," she says, "and I was amazed by it—all of those people there to see a car race. But we had a wonderful time. Mark showed me around, introduced me to a lot of racing people. It was all very interesting and exciting. I began to understand something about the life he lived."

That spring Martin proposed, Arlene accepted, and they were wed on October 27, 1984.

Matt, Mark and Arlene Martin after Mark won the Coca-Cola 600 in 2002. (photo by Action Sports Photography, Inc.)

picking him up. Doing 'mom' stuff. It keeps me pretty busy."

Arlene's hope is that the public realizes there is much more to her husband than just being one of the best racers in NASCAR history.

"He's a neat guy," she says. "He's not talkative, he's not easy to get to know, and people sometimes misread that. But he is a truly wonderful person. He has a lot of integrity and morals and values. That's the thing I most appreciate and love about him. Mark may be a great racer, but he's an even greater husband and father. He is a wonderful person."

> "I remember growing up in Arkansas and thinking that NASCAR was the coolest thing in the world and it was my dream to get there. I've been able to live out my dreams, and that means a lot to me. We've had a lot of highs and a lot of lows over the years, but I'll always be thankful for having had the opportunity to live out those dreams."
>
> —Mark Martin

(photo by Action Sports Photography, Inc.)

For the 1988 NASCAR Busch Series season, Mark made the change to drive for his friend from Arkansas, Bill Davis, who was making his first effort in the NASCAR Busch Series. Davis had secured sponsorship from a consortium of Ford Dealers throughout North and South Carolina. (photo by Dick Conway)

Mark drove limited NASCAR Busch Series schedules for Bill Davis and the Carolina Ford Dealers from 1988-1990. Here he speeds through turn four at Daytona in 1990 with his NASCAR Winston Cup sponsor, Folgers, taking an associate position on the car.
(photo by Dick Conway)

CHAPTER 5

The Son is Shining

They say the apple doesn't fall far from the tree, and in the case of Matt Martin that is especially true. Mark Martin's only child is a shadow of his father.

"My dad's my hero," says Matt.

Matt, like his father, began racing almost before he could see over a steering wheel, competing at New Smyrna Speedway. Now, at age twelve, Matt is a seasoned "veteran" with his own race car sponsors and even his own website.

"My goal is to someday be as great a racer as my dad," he beams.

Matt has never lacked for parental support. His father introduced him to Bandolero, Legends and Quarter Midget racing and even helped build a

track for his son and other young racers.

Matt got his picture on a Cap'n Crunch cereal box, signed a "development" contract with Ford and has his own website, mattmartin.net. The site carries this slogan: "Speed ... it runs in the family."

On his website, Matt treats readers to an array of racing photographs and such inside information as:

Favorite Bands: Linkin Park, P.O.D., Foo Fighters, Stone Age, All-American Rejects, Nickelback, Incubus.

What it's like to race a Legends car on bigger tracks: "It's fast. It's a lot easier to drive. I like the banking. It's tight."

(photo by Steven Rose/MMP, Inc.)

On playing football: "I'm probably going to play Pop Warner next year. My favorite position is halfback. I just like football. But none of that lineman stuff. I'm not fat enough."

On meeting Emmitt Smith, at the time a star with the Dallas Cowboys: "Meeting Emmitt was tight. He's a pretty cool guy. He's about 5-9. That's the size I want to be too, 5-9."

On visiting the Cowboys' locker room: "It was pretty cool, but it needs a Slushie machine. Some baseball teams have Slushie machines in their locker rooms. I was in the Pirates' locker room about two years ago and they have one."

On winning two track championships at New Smyrna Speedway: "I was the first in the 160 and first in the 120. It was pretty cool. The main deal is the Bandolero and Legends cars. The Quarter Midgets are fun, though."

On shifting gears in a race car for the first time (in his Legends car): "It was kind of hard to get used to, but [now] it's a piece of cake."

(photo by Steven Rose/MMP, Inc.)

Heading into the 2003 season, Matt listed what he considered his "career highlights" to that point:

• Tested Jeff Gordon's original Quarter Midget car at Charlotte Motor Speedway in 1998.

• Started racing Quarter Midgets at the age of seven, in 1999.

• Won the 1999 Mid-Florida Quarter Midget Racing Association Novice Championship.

• Drove in the Jr. Honda 120 class in the Mid-Florida QMRA and won four A-features and five heat races.

Matt's website also carries a revealing interview with Mark about his son:

Q. How special is your interaction with your son Matt in terms of keeping you in touch with what's really important in life?

A. "For people who might get tunnel vision about whatever they're doing in life, being able to do what I do with Matt and his racing keeps me in touch with what is truly important. It enables me to maintain a focus on what I'm doing with my career, but at the same

> *"I would love to be as big a hero in my son's life as my dad was to me."*
> **—Mark Martin**

time it makes you well-rounded, because there are a lot of other things in life that are important, too."

Q. The stories you've shared of your father's driving lessons on the front seat of a pickup truck were a precious piece of an irreplaceable time in life. Is there a parallel you can draw in your experiences with Matt?

A. "Today, it's a totally different time and not at all like it was when I was growing up. My father and I had a special relationship and a love for things that went fast. But today is completely different. Matt started racing when he was seven years old. I didn't start racing (competitively) until I was a teenager. I didn't even have a motorcycle when I was the age that Matt started at."

Q. Does Matt share the same enthusiasm of a young Mark Martin—and how do you relate to the experiences you had with your dad?

A. "Matt is not consumed by racing, as I was when I was younger. He is more diverse, and he has different interests than I did, in a lot of other things as well. From my perspective, I try to share and get involved in as much of that as I can. I feel that that's a benefit to both of us."

Q. Ford has signed your son to a development contract. As a father, that has to make you proud.

A. "I'm real proud of Ford. They're watching these guys on the race track and they're in the middle of signing a bunch of teenage drivers. They've got a great bunch of people out there scouting. The whole world of motorsports is changing, and it will be drastically different ten years from now because of the influence of the younger drivers coming into the sport."

Mark Martin fairly bursts with pride when discussing his son and his budding racing career. A couple of years ago after winning a pole at Bristol Motor Speedway, Mark devoted more of his press conference to talking about Matt than about himself.

"Matt really did good Wednesday night," Mark said, referring to one of his son's Bandolero races. "He won the heat race on a spectacular pass after he took the white flag. I didn't even know he had a chance to win. I thought he was going to get second, and all of a sudden he darted inside of the kid and won the race. It was pretty awesome. Then he finished second in the feature and ran a great race. Oh, man, it's so cool. I'm having more fun this year working with Matt than I've had since I was a kid."

> *"I love my son more than anything in the world, so I enjoy talking about him and I'm so incredibly proud."*
>
> *—Mark Martin on Matt Martin*

(photo by Steven Rose/MMP, Inc.)

(photo by Steven Rose/MMP, Inc.)

CHAPTER 6

The Cat in the Hat

Jack Roush is arguably the most familiar and colorful team owner in NASCAR, famous for his trademark hat and willingness to challenge convention and authority.

While Martin credits his wife, Arlene, for helping him get his personal life in order, it was team owner Jack Roush who provided the opportunity for Mark to revive his sputtering NASCAR Winston Cup career and molded him into one of the top racers in NASCAR history.

"Where would I be today without Jack Roush?" Martin says. "I don't know, but I'm pretty sure I wouldn't have enjoyed the racing success I've had. Jack has made all the difference in the world."

"Mark deserves all the credit," Roush says. "I just try to provide him a good car to drive. It's his talent and ability to drive the car that wins races."

Roush was born 62 years ago in Manchester, Ohio. He earned a degree in mathematics and physics from Berea (Kentucky) College in 1964 and completed his master's degree in scientific mathematics from Eastern Michigan University in 1970.

Roush developed Roush Enterprises, an engineering company with 1,800 employees world-wide and 50 facilities in five states, Mexico and England. But while he may be an international business tycoon, Roush's heart has always been at a racetrack.

Fascinated by all things mechanical, and especially by motors and speed, it was natural that Roush would become involved in racing. He formed a team, Roush Racing, in the early 1970s and

Car owner Jack Roush keeps an eye on things from the spotters' stand. At this time with only one team, Jack wears the sponsor's hat and not the brimmed hat he later made a trademark.
(photo by Dick Conway)

began competing—and winning—in a variety of drag racing and sports car series. His teams captured 119 road racing victories, 24 SCCA and IMSA championships, and the 1973 and 1974 NHRA and IHRA Pro Stock World drag racing titles.

Roush then set his sights higher, toward NASCAR and its premier NASCAR Winston Cup Series.

In 1987, Roush began laying plans to field a car in NASCAR Winston Cup the following season. He felt he already

Jack works on the car's engine at the June 1989 Dover race. Jack tuned the motors and works here with then crew chief Steve Hmiel. This was their first year in NASCAR Winston Cup, and Steve, Mark and Jack had just started the team from scratch.
(photo by Dick Conway)

had the mechanical and technical experience necessary to move into the big leagues after his vast and successful endeavors in other forms of motorsports. But Roush was wise enough to know that the best-built car is only as fast as the man behind the wheel, and he began a methodical search for the best driver available.

That search would lead to Mark Martin.

"I had heard about Mark and was familiar with what all he had accomplished," Roush says. "I kept hearing about how determined he was, how he was a fighter. That appealed to me. I consider myself a fighter, too."

In truth, Martin and Roush sought each other. Martin desperately needed a good ride, just as Roush desperately needed a good driver. Martin had heard that Roush, with major backing by Ford, was planning a foray into NASCAR Winston Cup, and Roush was already monitoring Martin's success in the second-tier NASCAR Busch Series. The more Roush watched Martin drive, the more impressed he became.

"What did I like about Mark? Everything," Roush recalls. "First of all, he was an extremely smart driver. He knew exactly what to do on the track at any given moment, in any given situation."

Helping Martin's cause was veteran mechanic Steve Hmiel, who had been working with Petty Enterprises and had agreed to join forces with Roush to build a NASCAR Winston Cup team. Hmiel discussed the deal with Martin

"When he came back, he was a different guy. He was more focused. He had a better understanding of what it was going to take to get to the next level of his career. He obviously had the gumption to do it."
—Steve Hmiel on Martin's comeback in 1987.

and promised to nominate him for the driving job. Martin anxiously waited for the call.

Finally in the fall, Martin told Hmiel he had to know something one way or the other. If he wasn't going to get the new Roush ride, he had to start searching elsewhere. Hmiel arranged for Martin to meet with Roush, and the rest, as they say, is history.

"We met and we talked about our goals and objectives, and then we shook hands," Martin says. "That was it. We had a deal. I'd start driving for Jack Roush next season."

Roush says he was sold on Martin for a number of reasons, starting with his obvious driving ability and keen mechanical knowledge. But, he admits, there was something else. Jack would say later on: "Hey, us little guys have got to stick together."

"Seriously, I do think that I probably had more empathy for Mark because, like me, he's not very big," Roush says.

Jack sits atop the pit box before the 1988 NASCAR Winston Cup race at Richmond. The gentleman to the right is Danny Bumpass, a Roxboro, North Carolina, Ford dealer who was instrumental in getting the Carolina Ford Dealers racing program started and who became a good friend and confidante of Mark. (photo by Dick Conway)

"He's out there racing against bigger drivers, and sometimes it seems like the little guys fight and scratch harder. As I talked with Mark, I realized that this was a guy who would fight and scratch to win races. I could tell that he was hungry, and I could see the determination in his eyes. He'd been knocked down, hard, and he was ready to get back into the fight. I realized that there wouldn't be a driver on the track who wanted to win worse than Mark.

"A lot of the other drivers I'd talked with seemed more interested in how much money they were going to make and so on. Mark? The only thing he wanted to know was when could we start winning races. I knew that I'd found my driver."

Robin Pemberton, another highly respected mechanic, joined Hmiel—who would serve as Martin's crew chief—and they began to assemble a team, build cars and test engines in preparation for their 1988 season debut.

For a brand-new team, the '88 campaign was not a bad one. Martin didn't win, but he earned a pole and posted three top five finishes in 29 races. He finished 15th in the standings and won $223,603, compared to $3,500 the pre-

vious season. Mark Martin's racing career was back on track.

"That was a very rewarding season, a big confidence builder," Martin says. "The more I got to know about Jack, the more I liked and admired him. I knew that he was the man I wanted to be with. I felt that we could go places together in this sport."

Every season since then, Martin has won over $1 million, and only twice has he finished out of the top 10 in the championship standings, slipping to 12th in 2001 and to 17th in 2003.

Jack Roush, the team owner referred to in NASCAR circles as "The Cat in the Hat," had indeed found himself a driver, and it was only a matter of time until he took that first monumental trip to Victory Circle.

It came at North Carolina Motor Speedway in Rockingham, N.C., on October 22, 1989. Martin, making his 113th career NASCAR Winston Cup start, started seventh in that afternoon's AC-Delco 500. He worked his way to the front, took the lead, and held it for the final 75 laps to beat his old ASA rival Rusty Wallace by 2.9 seconds.

All the hard work, the personal sacrifices, the wrenching setbacks—suddenly it was all worthwhile.

Martin pinched himself to make sure that he wouldn't wake up, a little boy back in Batesville, Arkansas, having a familiar dream.

In Victory Lane, Martin struggled with his emotions.

"I can't believe it," he declared. "My life is fulfilled. I feel I'm the luckiest man alive!"

Smiling proudly at his side was Jack Roush, who had helped make the daydream come true.

"I remember telling Mark to enjoy that moment," Roush says, "and to get used to it, because there would be a lot more like it."

Martin would not win again that season—despite five second-place finishes—but finished a solid third in the championship standings. Mark Martin and Jack Roush had erased any doubts that they belonged among the elite of the sport, although trials and tribulations still lay ahead.

At the end of 2003, Roush Racing had earned 66 NASCAR Winston Cup victories. And Matt Kenseth also won the NASCAR Winston Cup points Championship. Early in the 2003 season, he was asked about his climb toward the top.

"This is my 16th year in racing NASCAR Winston Cup, and that total was not something I had taken note of," Roush said as he headed into the 2003 season. "I have been in racing for 32 years, and we've won many, many championships in numerous series with programs that have been well exe-

> "What I said in Victory Lane is, 'My life is fulfilled. Every minute I've ever spent has been worth it now.'"
>
> —Mark Martin on his first career NASCAR Winston Cup victory in 1989

(photo by Action Sports Photography, Inc.)

cuted, well sponsored, well conceived and effectively promoted and utilized in the various venues.

"I take great pride in that. NASCAR is certainly not more than half of what I feel we have been involved with that has been worthwhile. In the modern era, we've got more than 200 victories, and that includes road racing and

NASCAR. The modern era for us started in 1984, but there were 15 years of serious racing before that, which is not counted in the totals we have on our wall of victories.

"The NASCAR victories are a source of satisfaction and pride, particularly considering the respect I have for Bud Moore [at one point Jack and Bud were tied in seventh place for NASCAR Winston Cup victories] and his contemporaries and my contemporaries today. As the totals roll up, that is certainly a source of pride and satisfaction to know we've been able to measure ourselves against people who have done so well and are respected so much, and say, 'We competed with them and performed with them.'"

Prior to the spring Coca-Cola 600—NASCAR's longest race, which was won by Martin in 2002 to extend Roush Racing's streak to four in a row—Roush discussed his philosophy concerning the lengthy events and offered some insights into the process that has produced so many victories over the years:

"If we do our business correctly, if we measure our risks honestly, and if we prepare as well as we might, then it doesn't matter so much if it's 400 miles or 600 miles. For the engine components that we test, we won't knowingly take something to a racetrack that won't last two and a half races. So if you've got a 500-mile race and we're testing a camshaft or some component that's expected to give you trouble, anything less than 1,250 miles would fail and you wouldn't take that component. You would take something that was known to be more durable, so

what winds up getting you taken out is something you hadn't counted on, and it will generally get you before you get 400 miles.

"Where there's an opportunity, if you're using your strategies correctly and you're figuring out what the race track needs, then you've got more time to react to things as the race goes on. You can start off further from the combination that you need, and as long as you don't have some component like a shock absorber that just doesn't function ideally, then you've got a chance to make the necessary adjustments like the track bar, wedge and tire pressure, and optimize your prospects. That's good, because it means you can race for a long time.

"I like 500-mile races. I like 600-mile races. I especially like 24-hour races. I like endurance races. We've had especially good luck the longer things run. If our stuff doesn't have a problem and we're as durable as we should be, then we'll be fine. I feel better about the 600-mile race than I do about the restrictor-plate races [at Daytona and Talladega]."

Roush said he tries not to get caught up in what he termed the "hype" of individual races.

(photo by Action Sports Photography, Inc.)

veteran, and Kenseth and Busch are considered two of the sport's budding young superstars. Biffle was a champion in the NASCAR Craftsman Truck Series and NASCAR Busch Series and is a driver from whom Roush expects great things in the future.

"I'm proud of all my drivers and proud of where Roush Racing is as an entity," Roush says. "A lot of people have worked very hard for a lot of years to get us to this point."

Jack Roush's Roush Enterprises employs more than 1,800 people worldwide, with 50 facilities in five states, Mexico and England. It has corporate sales of over $300 million.

Roush Racing won the 2000 NASCAR Craftsman Truck Series championship and the 2002 NASCAR Busch Series title. Going into the 2003 season, Roush's teams had engraved their names on 268 first-place trophies in the NASCAR Busch Series, NASCAR Craftsman Truck Series, SCAA Trans-Am, and ISMA GTO/GTS competition. However, Mark and Jack were both bursting with pride when Matt Kenseth captured the 2003 NASCAR Winston Cup Championship.

"It's been a blast," Roush says of his business and racing success, "and I predict there's a lot more in store in the future."

The Cat in the Hat is clearly a man who is enjoying his "bonus days."

> "Mark is a pillar of NASCAR. I'm sure that after he retires one day his career will be looked at by the historians and the fans as one of the 'greatest' of all time, regardless. Mark is one of the greatest to drive a race car, and time will show that."
>
> —Jack Roush on Mark Martin's career

(photo by Action Sports Photography, Inc.)

(photo by Action Sports Photography, Inc.)

CHAPTER 7
Teammates

To Matt Kenseth, Mark Martin is much more than a teammate at Roush Racing. Martin, Kenseth says, is his hero.

In the next breath, however, Kenseth confesses that—as much as he wants to see Mark succeed—he does his best to beat him every time they line up their cars.

"That's just the way it is in this sport, and Mark will be the first one to tell you that," says Kenseth. "He is a great friend and has been a tremendous influence on my career, but if we're both racing for the win, I'm gonna try my best to beat him—just like Mark is going to do his best to beat me. If he wins, I'll be the first to shake his hand, hug his neck, and congratulate him."

Such is the conflict of racing teammates, an association that has become commonplace in NASCAR's NEXTEL Cup Series. Single-car teams are virtually a thing of the past. Almost every successful team nowadays comprises more than one driver.

In the case of Roush Racing, there are five drivers in the stable.

Mark Martin is the veteran in the lineup, followed by Jeff Burton. Then come two sizzling young superstars—Kenseth and Kurt Busch. Greg Biffle, who had raced and won championships for Roush in past years in the NASCAR Craftsman Truck Series and NASCAR Busch Series, moved up to full-time NASCAR Winston Cup at the start of the 2003 season.

No team has a better blend of established veterans and budding young talent.

Mark and Matt Kenseth discuss strategy prior to the start of a
NASCAR Busch series race. (photo by Doug Hornickel)

Kenseth grew up in Cambridge, Wisconsin (population 800), just outside of Madison, where his father was a small businessman.

"He was involved in a lot of ventures," Kenseth says. "He sold furniture, ran a movie theater, and had a video rental store. As a kid I helped unload furniture and worked at the ticket booth at the theater. I was just a typical small-town kid."

On weekends Kenseth and his father attended stock car races at the local track, and Kenseth quickly became intrigued by the sport. His father bought him his first race car at age 13, and—like Mark Martin a generation earlier—Kenseth began to build a reputation.

Kenseth raced on the little short tracks sprinkled around the area, then began to branch out. He ran in the Hooters Series and ASA—where Martin was once so dominant—always dreaming of moving up to NASCAR Winston Cup.

"A lot of the races back then were on cable, and we didn't have cable at our house," Kenseth says. "My dad and I would go over to my grandfather's house and watch the races there. I knew that someday I was going to be out there with those guys, drivers like Mark Martin and Dale Earnhardt. That was my goal."

Kenseth made his NASCAR Busch Series debut in 1997, and that was the year that he caught the eye of Martin, who, in addition to his NASCAR Winston Cup racing, was also a dominant force in the NASCAR Busch Series.

"I liked Matt from the first time I saw him," Martin would recall later. "I liked the way he handled himself, both on and off the track. I could tell that he was a very talented young man who had a bright future in this sport."

Martin wanted Kenseth to have that future at Roush Racing. It was Martin who brought Kenseth to the team—he is officially listed as the owner of Kenseth's car—and he has helped nurture his career.

In 2002 Kenseth was the winningest driver in NASCAR Winston Cup with five victories, but a lack of consistency doomed his title chances.

Kenseth took a lesson from his elder—Martin—and vowed to work on his consistency the next season. He succeeded, taking the points lead early in the year and charging steadily toward the title.

(photo by Doug Hornickel)

Teammates Jeff Burton and Mark Martin. (photo by Action Sports Photography, Inc.)

"That comes from experience," Martin says. "We all want to win every race we run, but if you can't win, then it's important to get those top fives and top tens. Matt has done a great job of doing that. As I said, he's a smart driver and he learns quickly."

"Mark has guided my career," Kenseth says. "He helped me get where I am today. It's unbelievable that I've got this far this fast, and Mark is one of the big reasons for that. He's not just my teammate, he's my friend."

When Matt locked up the NASCAR Winston Cup Championship in 2003 Mark Martin was one of the first to stop by and congratulate him. Mark said, "I've been wrong about a lot of things in my life but I was right about Matt Kenseth. I'm real proud of that."

Jeff Burton is one of the sport's seasoned veterans, having broken into NASCAR Winston Cup racing in 1993 and collecting his first of 17 victories in 1997.

The native of South Boston, Virginia, insists he has no problem sharing the spotlight with Martin, considered the standard bearer at Roush Racing.

"Mark is where he is because he deserves it," Burton says. "He has been in the sport a long time and he has worked hard. I'm one of his biggest admirers. I'd do anything I can to help him, and I know he'll do the same for me. Being associated with Mark has made me a better racer."

Kurt Busch grew up in Las Vegas, but he says he was never part of the glitz and glitter of the city.

"My home was on the other side of the town from The Strip," Busch explains. "We were a blue-collar, working-class family."

> **"I'm personally thankful to him because he's a big part of how I got into Winston Cup and Roush Racing."**
> **—Matt Kenseth on Mark Martin's influence on his career**

As a youngster, Busch also was a race fan.

"Like a lot of kids, I was interested in racing, and my dad helped build me a car," he says. "The more I raced, the more I liked it. And I was having a lot of success. At a very early age I'd decided that I wanted to go as high as possible."

Busch was enjoying success in a variety of lower-level divisions when he heard that Jack Roush was "auditioning" drivers for a potential job with his team.

"I tried out and I felt like I'd done pretty good," Busch says. "Jack invited me up to his headquarters, we talked awhile, and he said he wanted me to start racing for him. I was on top of the world."

Busch made his NASCAR Winston Cup debut late in the 2000 season and collected his first victory at Bristol in 2002 just his 32nd start. He was the sport's hottest driver down the stretch in 2002 with two wins in the final five races and came out equally hot in '03. He finished 2003 11th in the points standings.

(photo by Action Sports Photography, Inc.)

Kurt Busch and Mark Martin. (photo by Action Sports Photography, Inc.)

Busch has already earned a reputation as one of the hot "young guns" of NASCAR, but he says there's another Busch who's just as good—his kid brother Kyle.

"He's the real racer in our family," Kurt said. "Keep an eye on him."

Greg Biffle had a career plan: win a NASCAR Craftsman Truck Series championship. Check. Win a NASCAR Busch Series Championship. Check. Win a NASCAR Winston Cup championship …

"I won't be content until I win it," says Biffle, a bright young driver who won his first NASCAR Winston Cup race at Daytona in July 2003, the Pepsi 400. "I feel that I have the ability, and Jack Roush gives me the car and the support I need to get it done. I realize it won't be easy, that I'm competing against the best race drivers in the world every weekend. But I'm in a perfect position, and eventually I'll make it happen."

As a NASCAR Winston Cup rookie, Biffle lost no time in making his presence known. He picked up a midseason victory and developed more and more consistency as the year wore on.

Roush says that presiding over such a diverse stable of talented drivers and fierce competitors—each determined to win every time he rolls onto the track— is not as difficult as it might seem.

"We have an understanding here," he says. "We're a team, but we're also individuals. We will work together to try to improve our total product and put the best cars on the track as we

possibly can, for each one of our drivers. But once the race starts, each driver and each team is an entity. I expect each to compete as hard as he can to win, and I try to support them equally. I'm thrilled for each of them when they do well because I know how hard each one, in his own way, has worked to get there.

"Each driver is special, just like each one is unique, and I'm proud of all of them."

In recent years there has been a flood of "young guns" into the sport; talented, ambitious young drivers anxious to stamp the mark of a new generation on the sport.

That means that every season, more pressure is applied to the sport's veterans, such as Martin, Bill Elliott, Ricky Rudd, Dale Jarrett, Ken Schrader, Rusty Wallace and Terry Labonte.

"It all started with Jeff Gordon," Martin says. "Jeff came into the sport and had tremendous success at an early age, and all of a sudden all the team owners were searching for the next Jeff Gordon—a hot young driver who they could train. These young guys are getting rides with great teams right off the bat.

Mark's teammates Greg Biffle and Matt Kenseth race for position. (photo by Doug Hornickel)

"When I came in, most team owners favored older, more experienced drivers. That's changed in recent years. If you're going to succeed in racing nowadays, you'd better get started early or you'll be left out. That's just the way it is."

A Charlotte pit stop in 1988. (photo by Dick Conway)

CHAPTER 8

"It Broke my Heart"

It has been well over a decade now, and it's still a sore, painful subject for Mark Martin: the 1990 championship that was lost on a controversial NASCAR penalty.

Ask him about it, and the blue eyes turn icy. The grin melts away. The lines around his mouth harden. It's not a subject he likes to discuss, even today. But it's also a subject he can't avoid: the one that got away.

It was 1990, and Martin came out sizzling. He won three races, including the second one of the season at Richmond. But in the wake of that March victory, Martin's car flunked a postrace inspection on what appeared to be a relatively minor technicality. A carburetor spacer on the engine's intake manifold was discovered to be slightly off-measure, according to NASCAR specifications. NASCAR

allowed Martin's victory to stand, but fined the team $40,000 and penalized Martin 46 driver's points.

That 46-point penalty would come back to haunt Martin. He would end up losing the championship to Dale Earnhardt by 26 points.

Team owner Jack Roush and crew chief Steve Hmiel insisted from the outset that the car had been inspected prior to the race and the thickness of the spacer was never questioned. They said it provided no advantage to the performance of the car.

"It's like rolling through a stop sign when nothing is coming, but a policeman catches you and writes you up," Martin says.

But the penalty stood, and in the end, it cost Martin the title.

Mark sits in his car just before a NASCAR Winston Cup race on a brutally cold day in February, 1990, in Richmond, Virginia. The day later turned even colder when Martin's car flunked postrace inspection due to a very minor technicality. He was penalized 46 driver's points for the violation and ended up finishing second to Dale Earnhardt in the championship by only 26 points. (photo by Dick Conway)

"You broke the law and you have to pay for it," a resigned Martin said, "but this is like getting the death penalty for running a stop sign. Was it fair? I don't make the rules."

Martin finished second in the championship chase three more times: in 1994, in 1998 and in 2002. The 1998 season was the best of Martin's career.

He won seven times—a phenomenal season in today's modern era when wins are harder and harder to come by—but Jeff Gordon had an even more remarkable run. Gordon won 13 races, relegating Martin's great season to second best both in terms of victories and championship points. His best was not good enough.

(photo by Dick Conway)

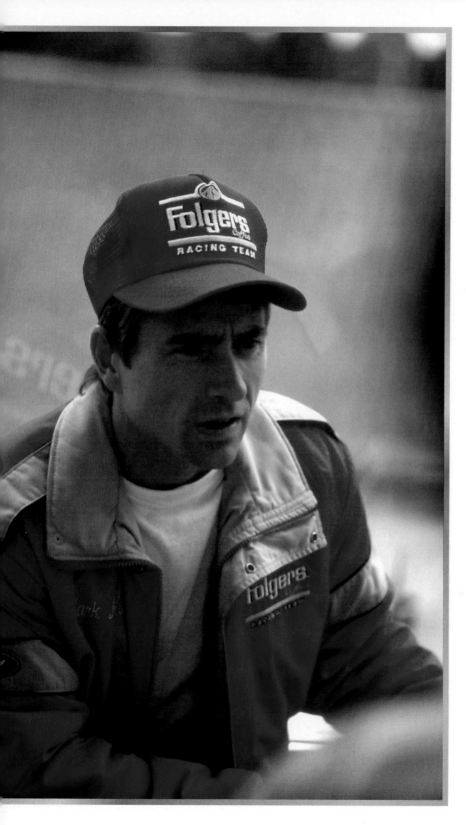

And after a close run, there was always the haunting memory, the nagging questions from the media, about the 1990 incident.

Martin tried to remain philosophical about the lost title, noting that the points penalty came early in the season and admitting that he had time and opportunity to overcome the setback. Indeed, with three races to go Martin held a 49-point lead over Earnhardt and continued to lead by 45 with two races remaining.

But in the next to last race, at Phoenix International Raceway, Earnhardt won while Martin came in 10th and Martin's 45-point lead was instantly turned into a six-point deficit.

After the dust settled on the season finale at Atlanta, Earnhardt was 26 points ahead. The crown went to Earnhardt, one of his record-tying seven championships.

"We lost it at Phoenix," a dejected Martin said afterwards. "We had the lead and weren't able to hold onto it. We don't have anybody to blame but ourselves."

(photo by Dick Conway)

Granted, there were a lot of races left after the early-season penalty. And yes, Martin had his chances to make up the penalized deficit. But the cold, stark numbers remained: A 46-point penalty and a 26-point defeat in the final standings.

Today observers still debate whether the penalty was just or unjust. Was it too severe? Was it warranted? Chances are that debate will never be resolved. But one thing that is not open to debate was its effect on Mark and his team: Heartbreaking. To have worked so long and hard and come so close ...

It's a wound that time has yet to heal.

The 2002 championship race began to look eerily like the bitter 1990 campaign after another controversial NASCAR penalty for an unapproved spring wiped out several of Martin's driver's points.

Martin's crew contended that the spring in question came straight out of the box from the manufacturer and had not been adjusted or tampered with in any way, but the penalty stood. Martin stoically absorbed the blow, but team owner Jack Roush, as is his nature, pulled no punches.

Going into the season finale at Homestead, Florida, Roush adamantly insisted that Martin's team was innocent of any wrongdoing.

As it turned out, the penalty was not the difference in Stewart's final total, as he secured his first title and forced Martin—for the fourth time in his career—to settle for second.

Martin had remained philosophical throughout the tense 2002 stretch run. Time after time he was forced by the media to relive the painful Lost Title of 1990. Martin didn't mince words, didn't try to disguise his hurt and disappointment.

"It broke my heart," he said. "I lived points hard that season, and I let it eat me up. Other than having to sell my race team, it was the hardest thing I've ever gone through in this sport. And you know what? There wasn't a thing I could do about it. So this time I vowed I'd never let that happen to me. That year [1990] I raced as hard as I could and I did everything in my power as a driver to win. I raced as hard as I could race. When you do that and still lose, well, you shouldn't hang your head and beat up on yourself. I did that once. I won't do it again. I know I've done my best, and that's all I can ask of myself."

Two former ASA drivers, Mark Martin and Rusty Wallace, race in a NASCAR Winston Cup race at Richmond in September of 1990.
(photo by Dick Conway)

In 1997 Martin went into the season's final race with a mathematical shot at the championship, but finished third behind Gordon and Dale Jarrett in the tightest three-way battle in NASCAR's modern history.

After each wrenching swipe and miss at NASCAR's brass ring, Martin kept his chin up.

"Getting down isn't going to help anything," he said. "You don't need to waste your time looking for sympathy in this sport. You're better off to spend your time and energy getting ready for the next race. If you don't win that one, you dig in your heels and try to do better the next one."

Martin compares the media attention devoted to his lack of a championship to that which was focused on the late Dale Earnhardt's long quest for his first Daytona 500 championship.

"For years all you heard about was 'Dale's failure to win the Daytona 500,'" Martin says. "Here was this great driver, with all those victories and championships, but nobody wanted to talk about all the races he had won; they wanted to talk about the one

(photo by Dick Conway)

he HADN'T won. I never understood that. Thankfully Dale finally won the Daytona 500 and got that off his back.

"What I've learned is that you can't control what people say or write. They're going to write what they want to, and it doesn't do any good to worry about it. I just ignore it and go on about my business. I don't pay any attention to it.

"Would I like to win a championship? Certainly. But I don't think my career—or any driver's career—should be judged strictly on that. Personally, winning races is still what's most important to me. If I go out every race and race as hard as I can race and do my best to win, then I can lay my head on the pillow at night and sleep well. I know I've done my best, and you can't ask any more than that from anybody."

A few years ago, the annual Motorsports Media Tour made a stop at Roush Racing's headquarters. Roush was holding court amid the assembled journalists when the subject of championships inevitably was broached. Roush's eyes flashed as he replied:

"We don't race for championships."

Later, he expanded on his comment, explaining that naturally he and his drivers would like to win a title, but that they can live—happily, thank you—by winning races in the absence of a championship.

He followed up on that philosophy in a recent interview:

"I may be a sucker for instant gratification. I'm able to tell before the [race] is over if we made the right decision on our gear selection and if we were able to react effectively to changes in the racetrack. I put closure on that and then prepare myself for the next challenge, which is the next weekend."

> "I have a hard time understanding how finishing second in the Winston Cup championship is a bad thing."
> —Mark Martin

Mark (in the Carolina Ford Dealers car) and a young Bobby Labonte (#44 car) at Dover in May 1990.
(photo by Dick Conway)

Translated: What's over is over—including lost championships. Don't waste time dwelling on losses.

"NASCAR has had a great program of championship racing, and it's celebrated a lot of champions for a lot of years," Roush said. "For reasons that have been well documented and are not comfortable to revisit, we have not been granted or graced with [a championship] and it's OK. I don't care. I'm doing the best I can and I'm happy with that. I've found peace and solace with myself and the way we run our programs and the efforts we've made. As long as I'm able to pay my bills and retain the amount of support and approval for what we do, then it's OK if I don't win championships. I don't care."

Still, it is apparent that Roush *does* care. He is an intensely competitive person who believes in racing hard and racing to win—whether it's racing for individual victories or season-long championships. And it's not just for him. Roush is extremely fond of Martin. The two have a virtual father-son relationship.

When Martin is denied a championship, Roush's heart aches for him—and for the tantalizingly close opportunities of the past. The specter is there.

(photo by Action Sports Photography, Inc.)

He said he doesn't mind that his car doesn't sport the label of some popular drink or cereal or mechanical gadget. Or the brand of engine oil that used to be painted on his hood.

He's happy with what he has, because what he has is a product that is doing something positive, week by week, for race fans.

Through the 2003 season at every race, a 50-foot mobile health unit owned by Viagra's manufacturer, Pfizer Corporation, parked in a lot near the track. It was called the "Tune-Up For Life" hauler, and it offered male race fans such things as blood pressure and cholesterol checks, and glucose tests.

"Just like everybody else, [Pfizer] was marketing a product at the racetrack," Mark explained. "They were giving race fans free physicals and health checks. A lot of these people wouldn't take off from work to go sit in a doctor's office to have a checkup. When you're over 35 years old, [you] need to be going regularly. And they weren't."

Martin, famous for his rigorous physical workouts and health-conscious living, was seen as a perfect spokesman for a product that promoted a "healthy living" campaign directed primarily at middle-aged men.

As Viagra's sponsorship of Martin's race car entered its third season in 2003, the "Viagra Racing Team" noted with pride:

"Thousands of people have received important health information because of this relationship. Mark Martin spoke to fans about healthy lifestyles on [various] race weekends, was featured in TV commercials, and made other personal appearances. Martin's Viagra TV commercial recorded the highest memorability ratings of any ad for prescription drugs in 2000.

"Pfizer's Tune-Up for Life continued to flourish in 2002. Another 35,000 people had received free health screenings when they closed the doors on this specially equipped mobile screening unit [at the end of the 2003 season]. This brings the total to more than 125,000 since the program began in 2000.

"Screening results from the Tune-Up for Life campaign in 2001 were compiled into abstracts for the American

(photo by Action Sports Photography, Inc.)

(photo by Action Sports Photography, Inc.)

mornings each week he is in the gym by 5:30 a.m., pumping iron.

"It's a great stress reliever, a way to work off excess energy," Martin says. "I got started years ago ... I just decided I wanted to get in good physical shape and stay that way. I work out, I watch my diet, I try to take care of myself. Does it make me a better race driver? I don't know; maybe. It certainly doesn't hurt to be in good physical condition when you're out on the track battling in the heat hour after hour. More and more drivers are starting to pay attention to that aspect of their lives, working and training to keep themselves in shape.

"I'm sure it helps me on the track, but the main reason I work out is because it makes me feel better about myself. I like the hard work, the discipline."

(photo by Action Sports Photography, Inc.)

(photo by Action Sports Photography, Inc.)

(photo by Action Sports Photography, Inc.)

(photo by Action Sports Photography, Inc.)

(photo by Action Sports Photography, Inc.)

CHAPTER 12

Into the Future

It's the age-old question for every driver: How does he want to be remembered?

Mark Martin squints his eyes against the glare of the track and ponders the query. A minute drags by. Then another ... has he forgotten the question? Then he answers, softly:

"I'd like to be remembered as a good racer," Martin says.

He continues:

"I know that may sound silly, but it's really that simple. In my mind, a good racer is someone who goes out on the track and gives his best on every lap in every race. He may not win them all, but to me that's not the only way you judge a driver. There have been some great racers who maybe didn't win a whole lot of races. Maybe they didn't have the equipment or the opportunity or whatever ... but they were still great racers.

"To me it's about heart and desire, dedication and determination. Willpower. Hanging in when times are hard. Not giving up. I'd like to think I've done all of that, and that people will remember it.

"There are drivers who have won more races and championships and so on, but I don't think any driver has ever tried harder than I have. I have never walked away from a race feeling that I didn't give my very best. I've fought and battled and ran my guts out. I've given it everything I could possibly give. That's how I hope people remember Mark Martin."

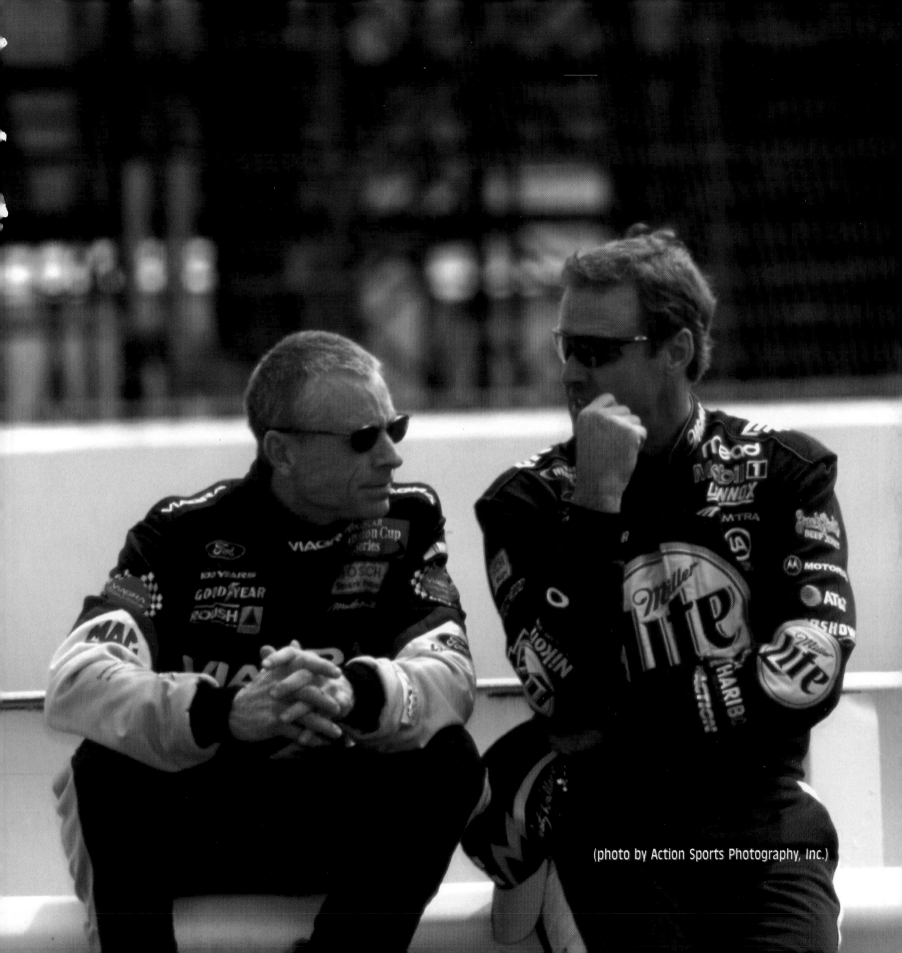

(photo by Action Sports Photography, Inc.)

"What do I think of when I think about Mark Martin?" says Jim Hunter, who has followed stock car racing for four decades as a sports writer, track manager and current NASCAR executive.

"When I think of Mark, I think about a driver with as much heart and courage and determination as I've ever seen. I've always had a tremendous amount of admiration for Mark because of his toughness. I've seen him trapped in the back of the field with a car that might not be all that strong in a particular race, and he would be battling for position—maybe 20th or somewhere on

(photo by Action Sports Photography, Inc.)

(photo by Action Sports Photography, Inc.)

(photo by Action Sports Photography, Inc.)

back—just as hard as if he were racing for the lead on the final lap.

"He's a guy who never gives up. That's the Mark Martin I've known for so many years."

Monte Dutton, a nationally syndicated motorsports writer, shares that sentiment:

"Mark is one of those drivers who will fight from the first lap to the last lap," Dutton says. "He's kind of a throwback to the old days when drivers didn't race for a lot of money or a lot of glory. They raced because it was in their nature to race. I think Mark Martin would drive just as hard to win a race on some little dirt track down in Arkansas as he would to win the Daytona 500. I really believe that. That kind of grit and fire is pretty rare when you think about it."

Says Darrell Waltrip, a three-time champion: "Tough. That's Mark. Tough as nails and ready to run the wheels off the car every time he rolls out on the track. There's never been a tougher competitor in racing."

Rusty Wallace, like Martin, is one of the sport's veteran drivers and an all-time great. Wallace and Martin came up through racing's ranks together,

> **"He's won all the races. He's won all the pole positions. He's done all of the stuff in Winston Cup he can possibly do, except win the championship. He's very deserving of it, and I hope one of these days he gets one."**
> **—Rusty Wallace**

competing in the ASA Series before breaking into NASCAR as eager, ambitious young lions. Because of their closeness, Wallace is able to offer a special perspective on his old rival/friend:

"There's never been a more determined, competitive driver in NASCAR than Mark Martin," Wallace says.

"Look in his eyes sometime at the start of a race and you can see it: the incredible focus, the will, the determination. I guarantee you, nobody races harder every second they're on that racetrack than Mark. He's a racer's racer and I admire the heck out of him. Beside the dictionary definition of 'race driver' they ought to put a picture of Mark Martin."

"I've been more successful than I deserve. I've had some of the greatest success a person should ever get to experience. Sure, I'd like to win the Cup, but I'm not going to lose any sleep over it because I've done all that I can do."

—Mark Martin

(photo by Action Sports Photography, Inc.)

(photo by Action Sports Photography, Inc.)

CHAPTER 13
The Statistics

Some of Mark Martin's career highlights:

- Won four American Speed Association (ASA) championships, 1978, 1979, 1980, and 1986.

- Made his NASCAR Winston Cup debut at North Wilkesboro Speedway on April 5, 1981, starting fifth and finishing 27th.

- Won his first NASCAR Winston Cup pole at Nashville Raceway on July 11, 1981, in his third start.

- Joined Jack Roush Racing full-time in the NASCAR Winston Cup Series in 1988, winning one pole and posting 10 top ten finishes.

- Named Driver of the Year in 1989 by the National Motorsports Press Association.

- Captured his first NASCAR Winston Cup victory at North Carolina Motor Speedway on October 22, 1989, in his 113th start.

(photo by Action Sports Photography, Inc.)

- Finished third in the 1989 NASCAR Winston Cup standings, after winning one race and six poles.

- Finished second to Dale Earnhardt in the 1990 championship race.

- Named to the American Auto Racing Writers and Broadcasters All-American team in 1990.

- Voted the top professional athlete of the month in August 1993 by the Pro Athlete of the Year Board.

- Won five races in 1994, including four in a row, and finished third in the standings.

- Finished second in the 1994 championship standings, again to Dale Earnhardt.

- In 1995 became the first NASCAR driver to win three consecutive races on the Watkins Glen (N.Y.) road course.

- Won four races in 1995, finished fourth in the standings.

- Captured four poles in 1996, finished fifth in the standings.

- In 1997 broke the NASCAR Busch Series record for victories with his 32nd win.

- In 1997 captured four NASCAR Winston Cup wins and was third in the standings.

- Won his fourth International Race of Champions (IROC) title in 1998, the most of any driver.

- Won seven races in 1998, the best season of his career, and finished second in the standings; also won the Bud Shootout at Daytona.

- Won two races in 1999, was third in the standings.

- Kept winning streak alive in 2000 with a victory at Martinsville, Virginia.

- In 2001 he posted his 293rd top ten finish.

- Finished second in the 2002 point standings for the fourth time in his career, challenging Tony Stewart for the title into the final race of the season. Won the $1 million Winston No Bull bonus with a victory at Lowe's Motor Speedway, boosting his seasons winnings to a career-record $5,279,400.

(photo by Steven Rose/MMP, Inc.)

Celebrate the Heroes of Auto Racing
in These Other Releases from Sports Publishing!

Jack Arute's Tales from the Indy 500
by Jack Arute and Jenna Fryer

- 5.5 x 8.25 hardcover
- 200 pages
- photos throughout
- $19.95
- 2004 release!

The Sands of Time: Celebrating 100 Years of Racing at Daytona
by Bill Lazarus

- 10 x 10 hardcover
- 192 pages
- photos throughout
- $29.95
- Includes a companion DVD!
- 2004 release!

Mark Martin: Mark of Excellence
by Larry Woody

- 10 x 10 hardcover
- 160 pages
- color photos throughout
- $24.95
- 2004 release!

Matt Kenseth: Above and Beyond
by Kelley Maruszewski

- 10 x 10 hardcover
- 160 pages
- color photos throughout
- $24.95
- Fall 2003 release!

Ryan Newman: Engineer for Speed
by Deb Williams

- 10 x 10 hardcover
- 210 pages
- photos throughout
- $24.95
- 2004 release!

Ryan Newman: From Purdue to Penske
by Deb Williams

- 5.5 x 7 hardcover
- 96 pages
- photos throughout
- $5.95
- 2004 release!

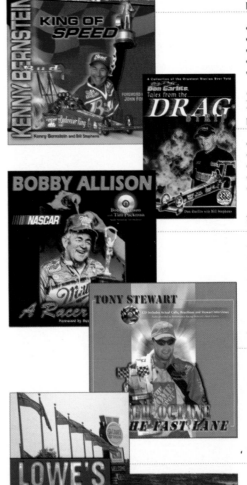

Kenny Bernstein: King of Speed
by Kenny Bernstein with Bill Stephens

- 10 x 10 hardcover
- 160 pages
- color photos throughout
- $24.95
- 2004 release!

Tales from the Drag Strip with "Big Daddy" Don Garlits
by Don Garlits with Bill Stephens

- 5.5 x 8.25 hardcover
- 200 pages
- photos throughout
- $19.95
- 2004 release!

Bobby Allison: A Racer's Racer
by Bobby Allison with Tim Packman

- 10 x 10 hardcover
- 128 pages
- color photos throughout
- $29.95
- Includes an audio CD!

Tony Stewart: High Octane in the Fast Lane
by *The Associated Press* and AP/WWP

- 10 x 10 hardcover
- 160 pages
- color photos throughout
- $39.95
- Includes an audio CD!

Lowe's Motor Speedway: A Weekend at the Track
by Kathy Persinger

- 8.5 x 11 hardcover
- 128 pages
- color photos throughout
- $24.95

Atlanta Motor Speedway: A Weekend at the Track
by Kathy Persinger

- 8 1/2 x 11 hardcover
- 128 pages
- color photos throughout
- $24.95